High Notes

Other books by Lois Roma-Deeley

Rules of Hunger

northSight

High Notes

poems by **LOIS ROMA-DEELEY**

This book of poetry presents a narrative based on some actual history, a lot of speculation, and much imagination. It is not a transcription or account of particular events or people.

09 10 11 12 7 6 5 4 3 2 1 First Edition
Paperback edition
Printed in the United Sates

Author photograph by Still 'N Motion Picture Co.
Cover photo by Tony Snow/Getty Images
Design by Claudia Carlson, www.claudiagraphics.com
Text set in Kepler Pro

Library of Congress Control Number: 2009939589

Publisher Cataloging-in-Publication Data
Roma-Deeley, Lois.
High notes / poems by Lois Roma-Deeley. —1st ed.
p. cm.
ISBN-13: 978-0-9815163-9-4 (pbk.)

1. Poetry, United States. 2. Jazz poetry.
3. Poetry, drug addiction.
I. Title.

**P.O. Box 5330
Hopkins, Minnesota
55343-9998
www.benupress.com**

for Peter,

Peter Michael Jr. and Melissa

Table of Contents

Setting

Late 1950s

Dramatis Personae

Harry Jones (age 45): hustler, drug dealer, loan shark, addicted to power and control

Jake Delmonico (age 34): jazz saxophone great; because he was driving high, his two boys, ages 3 and 6, died in a car accident; addicted to heroin and other mind-numbing drugs

Jasmine June (age 52): sometime blues singer, sometime waitress, nascent civil rights worker, addicted to sex and anger

Sugar Baby Hayes (age 27): blues singer, common-law wife to Jake, can't forgive Jake for being the cause of their children's death, addicted to alcohol, heroin and grief

Angel: spirit of grace and redemption, addicted to hope

Part One

The Minister of Rush Street

What, father, do you put into my hand?
—HARRY JONES

Be smoke rising from the iron grates of Rush Street,
touch no one.
Be the rattle in the brain of those who cannot sleep.
Be the bullet after it has left the gun.
Be the ship sailing into the mouth of a harbor;
the sea will fear you.
Be the roar inside the bird's stomach,
time will split in two.
Be lips upon the thighs of an unforgiving woman
who sings the blues.
Take this and
be the sum of all colors: pure white.
Be ice,
the cracking in the limbs of birch trees,
the heavy sound
in the forest of all that breaks and falls.
Be that refusal
which does not bow and will not weep.

After the Jam Session

CHICAGO, 1958

I.
Harry Jones Drinking Shots at the Bar

Give-it-to-me; give-it-to-me; give-it-to-me...
Nothing on earth is free.
Give—it—to—me; give—it—to—me; if you could only see

into these packets of white powder;
the eyes on the dice growing wider;

that cop's hand on your shoulder—
and your woman who is so much older

than you could ever be.
Now it's half past midnight blue...

and deep inside the snake eyes—
from beneath the hold of the saxophone—you rise

to find her; she is drinking gin, asking—
What should we do?
Now you will point at my alligator shoes.

And, oh, yes, the sweat on her skin will listen
to your cracked lips that whisper: *go home*
with him; this'll fix everything...

Now get down on your knees,
kiss the floor and believe

I will hurt you.

II.
Jake Delmonico, Jazz Man in His Dressing Room

Give ... it ... to ... me; give ... it ... to ... me; give ... it ... to ... me ...
my last taste of snow; my blue saxophone.

Act *as if;* act *as though*
these tracks on my arm
were put there to show
the way home. Don't you know

I owe
money to the man for ponies who land, head first, in the dirt—
they die—right before my eyes—inches before the finish line.
It hurts.

I owe money to the lady who cries about six months back rent.
With her hand in my back pocket, she moans:
I hear you have some work...

I owe the pawn shop for the pin I borrowed from my girl as she was sleeping;
she was breathing
easy, deep and low—you know—this is how it goes—
I didn't want to
shake her, wake her, ask her:
Honey, I need some money...

And—right after I see Harry Jones—
right after I drink a cuppa joe,
right after I cook this pure white snow...

the saxophone will cut the air
with blue notes, high and slow;
go now

be this what saves us.

III.
Jasmine June,
Counting Cash Behind the Bar

Don't tell me, I already know—
about *Jim Crow* and *Michelangelo*
about a winged lion and a diamond scorpio

that hangs around his neck. About the trick
of brass and strings
that will redeem us.

And yes, this is how it always goes
before each and every show.
After the music finally flows

into the trumpet, piano, bass and saxophone:
Give it to me; give it to me; give it to me...
The world can now start breathing. He is seeing

places I have stopped believing in—
Paris. London. Rome.
Where the Angels are made of rosy stone;

hollow eyes follow us, never leave us alone. So
shut off the radio. Hang up the phone.
Bring me a taste of pure white snow.

But now, as I count the quarters and the dimes,
I see the future, I have this feeling

a thousand wings are beating
against "Colored Only" signs...

this, our *some day, some time,*
this seventh heaven dreaming...

Give it to me; give it to me; give it to me

IV.
Sugar Baby Hayes, on the Stage With Jake

I hold my heart in my hand,
lift it
against my cheek. *Listen*
count the beats—

blood is rising:
A black woman and a white man

no one understands
where bone and skin begin
and end ... let's sing,

set the world on fire.

But this wish of mine
so color blind,
wants another
kind of ending.

Give it to me—give it to me—give it to me...

I trick the hours
with a silk flower
tucked into my hair—

it always works.

My backdoor man will be *my* church.
When I will kneel before him, I will believe
his every word.

Now the light inside my eyes is raw,
and every time the audience applauds

it hurts.

v.
Angel Waiting in the Alley

You won't see me,

in the white smoke of an uncertain fog,
You won't see me

in the street, lying down
beside a sleeping dog, waiting
in the alley for night to leave the dawn.

Not on the wind or in the rain;
not inside a bloody eye
or beside two clenched fists. No

you do not hear a word:

Give it over to me.
Give in, now, to me
Give it to me...

I am standing right here
where the air is cold and damp
and bone and skin are hurting.

Soon it will be enough
under this blue note of still sky
to open, slowly, both eyes and

say it, sing it, play it...

blind.

Sugar Baby in Her Grief

I am alone in my sons' room.

Wooden trains surround two plastic ducks.
Humpty Dumpty sits on the wall.

Under the twin beds, shoes lie in dust.
I wrap both wool sweaters—one brown, one blue—

around my neck.
Then I rock.

And the mattress screams from my weight.
But I rock and hum and

bury my face, deeper, into their clothes…

my baby boys…
I breathe them in.

The world does not stay the same, they say
but I say, *no!*

not now, not ever
I will never let you go…

What the Poor Know

When walking into an office, store or room,
I make my body thinner than a strand of hair.
When the manager/clerk/teacher looks my way
he/she sees nothing but a quivering line
vibrating in the air. I try not to breathe too much.
Always hold my chin in, tuck it close to my heart.
If the church woman in alligator shoes
comes to our house with bags of seedless grapes,
cans of lima beans, cartons of powdered milk,
I take it all.
She'll hand me a voucher from St. Paul's,
say my family should clean the yard, try harder
to find a job. I try not to think of aliens
who scoop out the soft spot of newborn babies.
At night, when I pray to God,
I try not to curse too much. But my eyes always drift
to the double holes filled with drying toothpaste
which are supposed to make
the screws of the screen door stay in place,
the flat tire in the living room that has to wait,
my aching teeth, that half-bottle of gin sitting on our floor,
the two dimes and twelve dollars I keep hidden
just in case.

Sugar Baby Hayes Fixing

If you are the needle, I'm the spoon—
There's no before and nothing comes after.
Here in the silence of the upper room

tie the ways and days of anyone who
separates the question from the answer—
If you are the needle, I'm the spoon

so smack the sides of jagged down to smooth—
the horse riding us, hard, is our master—
here in the silence of the upper room.

They say: you have to, you must, you will *choose*
to be the sun or the moon. It will go faster
if you are the needle, I'm the spoon

to pierce the heart of what they all assume—
listen, ghost children hang along the rafters.
Here in the silence of the upper room

we lost it all; there's nothing else to lose.
Enter the stillness, taste the dark that lasts—
if you are the needle, I am the spoon
here, in the silence, of the upper room.

Cover Story: Billie Holiday Traveling Into the Future

Her world is turning negative white.
It happens.
To be left on the back step after ringing the bell all night—
she wonders what others seem to know.
A doorjamb filled with fire,
was right behind her a moment ago.
She thinks *duck soup*
flaming in a silver bowl might be the more appropriate way to go
before the King. Or through the nose of hot pink elephants.

A chain link fence rattles a definitive no.
Riffraff begin to drift in
as whole notes pack up outside the theater window.
Three spotlights blind her eyes.
Standing dead center, she bows from the waist, waves to Elvis.

The only one who sees the star hunted by a crescent moon
and chased into a tree.   A kite
with a metal key is said

to attract electricity: the language
between them scatters underground.
Neon calls from the marquee: *If Only*
You'd Realize. Blasphemy

is just what it is. Yesterday the television showed her
who was among the chosen—
she alone would bring him back. That face, like the snowflakes of
late fall, vanishes

as soon as she hits the ground; eyes turned
to the white that once was

Graceland.

Slamming

This is how I enter eternity:
with a backwash of blood, the rush
of *now* in my veins.
These are not arms which will not hold
uncertain light. Swollen and bruised,
the sun will burn a door in the sky.
My head, nodding up and down,
gives its assent to heaven—

Jasmine & Jazz

Open me—
you will find a Sunday afternoon in Congo Square.
Slave ships. Drummers. Brass Bands. Creoles
in the street dancing memory
into my blood. You
who listen to this, listen well,
I never meant to forget them.
Those ghosts own me.
I do as I am told.

A Still Small Voice

No river with wide arms. No dry place high upon the trees. No trembling bit of asphalt cracking under the sun; no trainers with a whip and gun. Not the slight bright ring or angel wing pinned to a blue lapel. Nothing in the giant shadows cast onto the windows of a skyscraper. No form or shape. No saint to bless by name. Not on TV or beside the street preacher. Not under blue awnings or inside rose tattoos. No fires are left burning. No Elijah waiting in the voting booth, breaking into a long speech. Just this standing inside the here and now, the whistle of *listen, listen, listen*

Arguing With Angels

It is the August thunder storms that speak
for me. The voices from outside of time
will press their lips to both my cheeks and weep,
What do you want? "Just give me what is mine,"
I say to threads of silver dust that cling
to shaking window shades. *What will you have?*
How can they answer blood and bone? *Nothing*
to say? the dancing echoes spin and laugh
at me. I may not own the heart that pumps
uncertainly inside my chest, or holds
my breath within or lets it go; but what comes
through yellow rooms to open me is cold.
It drinks the rain; it asks, "How will you live?"
I make my hands a cup: *with only this.*

Jake Delmonico's Broken Time

I.

There are planes waiting at airports to be
filled with people who look like I should know
them…curled inside red chairs, jazz men
snore; bubbles forming in the corner of their open
mouths. *Ornette?* I say and

II.

he gives me that look. I play him a song. Then he
pulls down my hat, it covers my eyes. *Tomorrow Is
the Question!* crackles through a broken radio.With
hands touching the side of his thighs, he sighs—a
parenthesis of reason. Now, he draws close,

III.

closer still…with the top of a bottle of gin, he
taps my heart: *Would you really call this art?*
Now there are the cities printed on laminated
maps circled in black. Mountain ranges that
chant: *Isn't this what you were supposed to
do?* Yesterday …

IV.

Sugar Baby fell into a circle of light. She tucked the
silk rose into her hair, started singing… Now in the
back room of this old motel, I am packing my gig
bag. In the next room, Jasmine knocks, three times,

V.

on the wall, cries: *The silver locket with the snips of*
hair—the one I always wear—cannot be found.
Her gambling man took it from her when
she was sleeping. When the winter wind was
weeping. Last night he pressed his lips to

VI.

her hips, whispered: *I swear—no more—no*
packets of China white; no more fists and
broken windows…no late nights with dark
ponies. I swear by all that's holy. Now she
falls to the floor; bites the back of her hand.

VII.

He's gone. I turn off the light. Sugar Baby turns in bed.
Her fingers grip my shoulder. Now she has to
know: *Who sold my very own antique watch and*
pin? Who wrapped it in blue tissue, put it to one
side? Now there are clerks in the supermarkets

VIII.

of small towns on the edge of big lakes who make
change and talk wise about husbands who are,
after all, only men… But I am dreaming every
night. Of Versailles—and my sons who died. Of
Sugar Baby and of falling snow. Of Archangels
sent to test us

IX.

at every turn of the highway, in every gas station, juke joint and smoke-filled bar, inside every toll booth and slow moving lane of traffic. In smoke-filled rooms. In slamming doors of my green *Bel Air.* Of cities growing deep inside...

At Minton's, New York, 1958

The brim of a fedora hat.
Snap like that.
Pearl earrings. Minks and fox.
Too hot…not to trot.
Smoke rising from a dozen candles.
Rap the table.
Whiskey. Cigarettes. Float across the floor.
More and more.
Lips against an ear.
Let's get out of here.

Jasmine Waking in a Cheap Hotel

DETROIT, 1958

She stretches,
        pulls at the peeling paper
just above her head. She lifts her thumb,
        closes one eye. It's certain
these faded peonies on the far wall hide inside themselves
        only to bloom at night.

This man in the bed next to her—what *is* his name? *Mitchell?*
        Michael? Miles?
The sun pushes through a hole in the curtain,
        curses them all
with too much yellow light. She turns over,

watches the man's chest
        rise under the cotton sheet.
Last evening at the club, his music
        split her in two. She liked how
he moved on the stage—a big cat in a cage.
        Later, his teeth would sink into her
and she would feel whole.

In the distance, she hears the 12 o'clock siren wail:
        get up, go home.
Suddenly, she is sixteen years old.
        It is the winter she met Harry Jones. Those days
opened her…saxophones, reefer, torch songs, promises.
        She still believes in love.

She remembers her mother standing over the stove,
    singing *Amazing Grace* into a pot of boiling soup,
her cheeks going shiny from the rising steam.

    Don't be late…

Mama always pointed at her with a wood spoon,
    then pointed to the kitchen door,
slapping the air with each word:
    a-man-won't-buy-the-cow-if-the-milk-is-free.

Now sipping gin from a dirty glass—she gets up, looks into the street.
Now across the bathroom sink,
she stares into the mirror,
    nods, tries to smile
at the tangled hair, drooping lids, double chin.

Her hand cups her breast.
    It's round and firm.
Still young.

Confession: An Angel Answers Art Pepper

You lean both elbows on the sill.
It's winter. The day is growing dark.
Tracing a star
into the circle your breath makes on the glass
you stop. Something
like the wind is reaching for you.
There are no footprints at the front door.
Snow is shoved against the sides of the street.
Voices shout from another room.
You think you know them—
the familiar arc of speech, slurred words,
the syntax of desire.
If this were not your own life, it would be romantic:
the sun setting into the snow,
the snow turning orange in the cold,
blue notes on a saxophone,
tracks under your tongue, between your toes—
You sigh—
just outside this window there is a field
which stretches to a small lake.
There ghosts hang from winter trees.
Their eyes are open. Their necks, broken.
The wind confesses to the sky:

So be it

Part Two

Not Here, Not There

JAKE DELMONICO

I am afraid of dark eyes in the mirror.
Of you waking and seeing me nodding in the big blue chair.
I am not afraid of dinner time,
of men who show their women the hairy backs of open hands.
I am afraid of cockroaches, the A-Bomb, oncoming lanes of traffic
        roaring down my spine—
My horn in the pawn shop.
The forgotten faces of our children.
I am not afraid I am out of the luck I never had.
Or the last unremembered kiss—
of that morning when gin in a tall glass refuses to steady you—
I am afraid I am that man who finds strangers for you, brings them home.
I am terrified of the sound a zipper makes.
Rough fingers between your legs.
Of voices at our door.

Harry Jones Holds School

Now take some note. My words are true. These days
of hunger greet you like a lover who waits
to close your eyes. With heavy sighs, you say
oh no, this too…was nothing. Fingers shake
the needle, cook the spoon; the neon red
inside your head now opens. Read the line,
the crease which is a life, the single thread
of getting up, then out of bed… I'm *right*
beside you. *Stop.* Now bring to me whatever needs
undoing. Knife the edge; kill the shadow—
that impulse rising far from simple feeling.
Released into a winter fog I float
Through window, door and sky. You're so concerned….

I am the lesson last to be unlearned.

Flying

ANGEL

1.

Look down.
Through the scrim of clouds,
a cow is chewing grass and
dreaming of cool springs
running beneath the earth.

2.

Look down.
Across the wide field, there is a run of mud
upon which wood boards sit
leading to a blue house built on a hill.
A rush of troubling sparrows
flit, high, into the trees, hide
in the leaves—
They bear no witness.

3.

Look down.
On the floor of a room,
a man lying on his back
closes one eye, stares
through the "v" of his forefinger and thumb
which frame the bare bulb hanging
above his head.

4.

Look down.
The halo of light
around the winter moon
is a rune of snow.

5.

Look down.
Your heart
is beating inside your chest,
a trapped bird
flying, again and again,
against the glass
of a closed window.

Chet Baker: By Instinct and With No Regrets

Everyone thought I was dead: a vagrant drowned in the sound.
It was myself, my woman told me later,
who spoke from deep inside of sleep,
of a man dressed in a yellow raincoat.
The surveyor of dreams. The one who stands near the edge
with telescope and spirit level
pointed toward the small gulf which separates us
from the city.

I had been walking for days in my sleep, trying to find
where shadows green the deep of sea.
Heard webbed wings, kept seeing things,
flying under the cantilever bridge. Pterodactyls soared into the blue
iris of my eye. Time was

two women digging with a teaspoon.
Soon there will be a thousand steps carved into the mountainside,
each the length of a lady's arm
resting on a table.

At day break clammers trawled the bay with iron tongs and wire nets.
They pulled both arms into their chests
and picked the seed beds clean,
calling it *even*
between us. The creatures retreated
when the women came with their silver spoon.
When it was high noon. When the sun burned

the backs of his hands—and his hands,
freckled and peeled deep red, finally stop shaking.

The Visitation of Angels

KANSAS CITY, 1959

I.

The window above the sink rattles. Pots and pans shake.
Two lovers sit at the kitchen table, stare into each other's faces...

So Sugar Baby has learned to rub the cat's paw,
crack the back door—just enough—to let the ghost pass.

Then Jake will believe her when she tells him
"it's the hole in the ozone

drifting over the Mojave desert
that sucks up all the air, that shatters all the glass."

Not you, Harry Jones. Not your tongue
rolling ice cubes over in your jaws...

like the bones of field mice ground down
by indifferent molars of a grizzly bear. Jake groans.

Now, from deep inside the forest, dead leaves fly
over the frozen lake. She breathes in;

II.

yellow walls grow thin.
The night, at last, holds still.

Beneath Sugar Baby's seat,
black roses harden on a linoleum vine.

Jake dozes, sees a picture
painting itself into the corner of his eye:

A rusting truck. A track of country road;
Red dust on his left shoulder.

He is weeping ...
the barrel of his own gun hits the sides of his back teeth.

Now you step away from this scene. Your hand is open
and unforgiving.

I rise,
tap the ceiling with my head.

Sugar Baby says: "Wait a minute...
It isn't money or a place to sleep...

III.

is someone speaking?"
It's not a top hat, cane and dancing feet.

"Who is it?"
I float across the room. You know

how Sugar Baby looks when she moans
into the bottle, wishing it held more gin. Jake doesn't want to think

about the notes he has to coax from his saxophone.
He fingers the keys, tastes the reed, inhales

and the door closes.
Now, finally, they're alone.

IV.

Later we'll hear sun
screaming through squares of glass.

Sugar Baby lifts her head, listens.
Just give in…

Jake gets up. She grips the side of her chair.
Please…please…

Now, Harry Jones, you get up to go.
Sweetness is drifting into the hollow of Jake's arm;

I am settled in the limbs
of the winter trees surrounding this old house and farm.

A fist of wind
knocks against the door of this old kitchen. *Look*

On this day beneath the eaves, on the ground, in the snow,
these words are being written:

no one ever has to know.

Jasmine Watches the Little Rock Nine on TV

I am a black woman yelling at the white man
inside the TV set which hangs over the bar
like a possum in a tree… *These are only children…*
I wipe the counter hard. Then wipe it again, slapping the surface
with my rag. The wood is smooth.
…*they just want to go to school.* Now I am counting my tips,
thinking of the last time I left home…
How my little brother begins to stutter
every time Mama grabs his arm and whispers:
Emmett Till.
Blood runs down the side of her comb.
The boy holds very still.

Getting Sick

The phone refuses to ring.
It's a demented thing.
Did you take your wedding ring?
Is the pawnshop still open?
My mother keeps a little cash
in a canning jar behind the last
of this summer's
sweet tomatoes.
What time did he say—did he say?—when I can get over?

Not Yet a Junkie Whore

SUGAR BABY

I am afraid of the air
between midnight and
noon—afraid of running
out of cigarettes and
running out of booze. I fear
the collapsing blue sky
above my head, the empty
needle, the bastard
spoon…and pawned rings
and stolen checks. I am
scared of shoes that slide.
Men without faces. Black
and blue eyes—heat that
rises in the middle of
July… I am afraid of what I
won't do in strange beds in
distant rooms.

Sister Friends

JASMINE TO SUGAR BABY

Inside my house, you watch the ceiling ... listen
for whispered storms that twist within. We know
the sweaty palms of angels clapping rend
and crack the sky. You hush me. Now the slow
unfolding wings of peacocks dancing round
both houses seem to me to be a sign
from God. The tulips' heads are bent. The ground
beneath us swells in waves. The orchard vines
you planted near the door begin to trill:
It should be written on the wall. To what
upturned face should we turn? And not be killed
by love? For this that rises in us cuts,
divides in two: we are the quick and dull
afraid of breathing, deep, the storms to come.

Downtown Jake

The packet on the table sits next to the syringe.
Inside my pocket,
a fist clutches all my change. Two dimes. Five quarters.
I am counting the days
since we got straight. But there, right in front of me,
is just a little taste.
This is on the house... Harry Jones says...*for old time's sake.*
My woman, standing at the door,
lets her eyes sink
into the back of her head.
Pick up the needle; pick up the spoon...
Her tongue, dry inside her mouth,
sticks on each word. *This-is-*
the-very-thing-I-need... *I need*
this...her voice is climbing now, the sound rising
from the gravity of earth, the noise breaking
over each syllable—then
finally, I am drifting

on a ribbon of wind, rushing
through a narrow alley of an empty street; I've become the snow angel
rising to greet children,
the lullaby inside the throat of a sparrow. Now I am
the hush in the head
too heavy to lift itself from the chest,
I am the stillness
between grief and sorrow.

Walking to Her Day Job, Sugar Baby Contemplates Her Dead Children

In green and yellow swirls, I see the walk
I take to work each day start to bloom.
Cement glows now beneath my feet.
These scrawls the children make—their world of giant moons,
balloon faces, sad aardvarks, and bouquets of daisies—rise about me…
often I blink and see my boys among the chalky hay and bales of wheat…
just say the sun *shrinks* this time of season…
Oh! I'm late.
As this unpainted door swings open,
now I stop and step into the shop.
I'll tear these strips to ribbons.
This, my art and craft—
the knot that holds the silk to flower—stands in wait…
for love believes in whatever it makes.

Cabaret Card

JAKE

Into the rainy dawn of a New York Saturday,
a flock of pigeons fly
on a cold arc of air. Before they can return to their coop

on the roof of the Blue Haven Café, a door will open.
This will be the day the red flash

of police sirens pulses in small rings
on the water pooling in the street. Inside

the smoky room, a saxophone has been playing.
A woman has been singing

dream notes—the sound rising
inside the wanting

of some familiar thing
lost long ago.

Now an officer makes the arrest,
his finger pointing to the white packets

spread out on the desk. I could say, yes
this was when

the birds' sly wings would stop fluttering
inside their roof top nests. Or when

on the back of the west wall and
in my half-closed eyes,

I heard these words being written:
you-will-never-work-again.

Bird Talk

Jake is at the pawn shop. The door is about to close.
His horn nests in a hole of torn wool, grown large under the left arm
of the last wool jacket he owns.

This seemed like a good idea: buy a ticket
for New York, Paris, Rome—

Across the street, birds talk
among the leaves:

be the rippling not the stone—
be the whisper inside the ear
be the train and not the station

be intention

be the green beneath the sun
be the book and not the words
be that rest between the notes

be fluid and harsh—

be large

be the rising within a moan
be the step and not the shoe
be the ringing of alarm—

the wind inside the throat—

be opened

Part Three

Light From Distant Hills

A stack of paper falls to the floor.
There is no other sound in the house. It is the midnight of winter.

Pearl cameos of two children fill the frame
of this kitchen window. From the ceiling

I have been watching him for hours.

Light from distant hills
flickers. Someone is about to sleep.

Are we there yet? Are we?

His boys' voices, rising and falling in the back seat of his Buick,
were smooth as ice on the city road.

And he never did feel the wheels jump,
the tires skim and float into the next lane.

Now, he smells the side of a whiskey-soaked cigarette
and sighs. He decides to close his eyes

for just a little bit. The spike is still in his arm.
Blood is staining the walls.

Are we there yet?

Tomorrow he'll play
the last set. He'll step inside the high notes,

but his legs won't hold. The music will break
and he'll fall into the crowd.

Then I will lean over his body
slumped against the stage and whisper:

come home.

Alligator Shoes

ANGEL TO JAKE

Beyond this river which runs through the city and
the wild woman who stands weeping
over an open grave, there is a house.

But you are not sleeping in a yellow room
on the second floor, dreaming of alligator shoes
and the deep blue of lilacs. You are walking down

Rush Street. Because you are cold and alone
and certain no one will hear,
you sing out loud, making up words

with each step. It is a song about wanting
but not getting. About brown eyes and gray smoke.
About rain falling as a full moon rises

through an open window. Two lovers who
fall into dreaming. You hope
there is such a place

back in the country house
where a woman will take the back stair,
the wood moaning under the weight of both feet—

As she floats down the hall into the room
of your children, her hand will smooth the rough ends
around the sheets. Then, at last, she will come to you—

between hard and sudden beats
of freezing rain—now this woman will forgive
you, you
who don't know how to live.

Deleted Scenes From an Attempted Suicide

JAKE: LOS ANGELES, 1959

1.

I should have been more careful, should have
listened when they said:
Look away. Look out the window.

2.

A fire truck stops in the middle of the street.
Men in hip boots and yellow jackets break the front door.
Someone hooks a ladder to my second story window.

3.

Down the street, on a grassy hill,
a young girl is singing to the sky.
She is dancing in the breeze. She is dancing with her cat.

4.

A neighbor runs across my front lawn. He carries an ax.
Now I lie on the floor,
stare at the ceiling. I am thinking

5.

it was still early evening
when I sat down at the long table, put the linen napkin in my lap,
drank *Pinot Grigio*

6.

not gin from a tall glass. Last night
I ate fire roasted peppers and New York steak.
When I picked up my spoon, turned it over,

7.

my face stretched across the silver moon. The nose was thin.
The eyes, too narrow. I read the lips:
never tell anyone

8.

about the girl who sings.
She is waiting to speak.
She is waiting for me.

9.

Now I am crouched in the window. The wood frame taps my back.
Below, the crowd opens its mouth.
I turn

10.

and there you are filling the doorway.
Two days from now
you will come to our old house.

11.

I will be sitting in the plain chair.
You will knock. I will say
come in

12.

You smile at me. I smile back.
Putting three pills in a blue plastic cup,
you place them before me. Then,

13.

remembering *fire-girl-singing-cat,*
I pound the table, clench my jaw.
Between my teeth, I swear

14.

on the grave of my two sons: *never again*
ignore the voices
who tell you

15.

jump

Sugar Baby Kicking

Like this. No one said it would be like this.
Yawning tears, and diarrhea—my skin is
itchy and my stomach hurts—I would like
to leave—please—let me go—when, tell me when
will the pain stop? It's really too much and—
I need something. Get me something—right now.

There's yellow paint peeling off the walls. Now
that bitch across the hall is screaming: *this*
demon-witch wants to eat my heart out and—
then she looks at me ... a terror; *come on* ... is
there anyone who can help me?—Tell me when
can I go home? When at times it gets just like this

my leg and hand they throb, go cold, it's like
the rat's teeth chewing straight through to bone—now
you know I'm not a junkie? It's just when
my man doesn't come home and he has this
far away voice on the phone and he is
telling me he just got lonely—that—and

when the bills just can't get paid—the rent and
the loan payment are late, it just seems like
we should quit trying. Don't tell me what is
not possible. And what should I do now?
After the sweating, after the puke, this
is the moment of maybe, not should, when

you say: *perhaps it's time to go*—Oh! when
can I go? What do you know? The world and
its hungry belly never get full. This is
how I live—I make the soul numb—like
a scorpion's sting, the stunning now
shuts down and I am Queen of all that is

in front of me. Not the nothing that is
spinning around me, whispering how this
or that—person or place or thing—is now
a thumb on my neck, whip at my back and
even the hole in the hospital wall is like
a grave I should just fall into. All this—
—you think I like being *like this?* And is
there a sign for when it will end? Like if
my heart could stop the desire of *now this.*

Maybe and Because

JAKE

Up and down. Across and around. Wet rag over wood bar. Glass circles. Notes of another country. *Cold cold.* So my thoughts of you. *As if* in snow. *As if* the blue sky on a pond. Shadows and silhouettes. *As if* a rose quartz eye. *As if* your idea of me: swans at the edge of a wide-mouthed lake. Green moss at the base of this unremembered rock. Sighing in the streets. Underneath this continuous stream of *what* and *how* and *when*—you and me?—*who*? Before the King of *What If.* After the Queen of *Suppose.* Why? Now *assume* aquamarine. Blue Moon. Bluegrass. Blue plate special. Blue whales. Baby blue. Blue baby. And you. *Oh! Sugar Baby.* Shoes under our bed. Two for the movies. Now presume a rabbit hole. Down and around and through. Threads into clothes. Nail heads around a couch. *Maybe and because.* Glasses along the sink. Between the sea blue and the steel blue, thoughts of you. *Blue Haven.* Lupine light. Teeth between two lips. Now ice blue. Deeper. Go deeper... Arms. Neck. Shoulders. Waist. Drift into space. Going down. Gone under. Stone and Fate. Disappear under your own weight

Jake in the Desert

This is where the car breaks down,
Sugar Baby always says
in the middle of the story about how her family
came to live in a house
made of fake adobe and how, every Christmas,
luminarias, which line the sidewalk of St. Maria's, *flicker*
before burning out; the wick of
each candle hissing against the wind. We must
put salt on the tongue
before she can speak the names
we chose, the ones we lost...

Those boys who died so young.

Side Slipping

Leading you through the long field, past the haystacks
someone is singing, Harry, only to you.
Her red hair falls onto her wings.
The silk gown slips down her shoulders,
uncovers the tops of her breasts.
You think her voice is like your mother's
after waking from a deep sleep.
Harry, do you think the world difficult?
Or just this scene?

Improvisational Memory

JASMINE

He sees me sipping coffee in the square.
This would be spring. It could be Rome. The book
of lotus petals closes. Now the air
belongs to sudden rain. He stares. I look
at clouds that float along the fountain's edge.
The winged lions open, wide, their mouths
as if in mock surprise. He holds the pen
my mother gave to me. My man sits down
and untied pages fly out—one by one—
across the street. *I have nothing to say.*
Now marble heads are turning. Pigeons run
after the crumbs you feed them. Every day
as I wait here before these rings of blue,
the water asks me: *now what will you do?*

{ Perfect Music }

ANGEL

The cigarette is floating in a glass of whiskey,
and not far beyond it, the glimmering saxophone
collects the gray smoke of drinkers.

It is near dawn.
A waitress runs a rag along the bar,
puts up the stools. Her apron smells

of rose water and cedar. I am remembering
the day her voice gave out,
how the doctor said

what did you expect? Her figure
was next, the breasts and hips
making a flawless pear.

The diamond around her neck
was all that was left when her husband died.
Suddenly she smoothes her hair,

placing a strand behind one ear.
There is music floating through the air.
I am standing right here

but she doesn't see me.
I am standing with my hand
on the microphone.

The sirens in the street are rising.
She recognizes the sound
as something whole, perfectly round—

the ghost of high notes
touching the face of a late night sky.

Retreat for a Blue Monk

Say it is a child's wish, this wanting and wail:
to be captured by the snare drum; to pass through
the snapping jaw of brass cymbals;
to slide down the throat of a horn—
head over bent knees—to live inside the trumpet's stomach—
where, after a mighty heave, I am reborn
with a caul and blue beret.

The Biography of Now

No point, the Angel will tell us, not even a dot.
But there was a dot, though we couldn't find the place
except we dream it. The place on the map of time
to put a finger on. That is, the imperfect now
opens and, in that opening, the Angel stands and waves to us.
And the waving is like a rising ribbon of light. And the light
is a road on which we step. And in the stepping—
the lifting of the foot, the foot set down into the dust—
we are moved.

When Sugar Baby Sings

Like a cat's eye in the sun.
Like gravel under a taxi wheel.
Like confessions inside a cathedral.
Like passing dope around the table.
Like pouring water into a tall glass.
You go as morning and return at night.
You go as shadow and return as light.

Back Door Man

With a stick
I found along the shore,

you are writing
our names in the sand.

We both measure time
by lengths of string

we put in a bottle,
throw the bottle out to sea

—wait for the language
we've come to understand

as sun over water,
water over sand.

We stand at the shore
digging in our heels

pulled by the tides
of each continent.

All winter
we called this ocean home...

Now I
fill a cup with sand.

The waves come in,
and then go out...

Our names fade.
What story can contain us?

Acknowledgements

These poems—or versions of these poems—were published in the following:

"A Still Small Voice" (first published as "Tickets and Keys") *Artful Dodge;* "Chet Baker: By Instinct and With No Regrets" (first published as "By Instinct and With No Regrets") *The Oregon Review;* "Cover Story: Billie Holiday Traveling Into the Future" (first published as "The Homely Modest Pale") *The Midday Moon;* "Downtown Jake" (first published as "The Aria of Jazzman Jake Delmonico") *Paterson Literary Review;* "Maybe and Because" *5AM;* "Jasmine Waking in a Cheap Hotel" (first published as "Waking in a Cheap Hotel") *Studio;* "What the Poor Know" *Superstition Review.*

In the 2009 Allen Ginsberg Award in Poetry Competition, "The Aria of Jazzman Jake Delmonico" was selected as an Editor's Choice Award winner and published in the *Paterson Literary Review*. In addition, "Arguing With Angels" was paired with the visual art of Beth Shadur and the music of Christopher Scinto as part of *Collaborative Vision: The Poetic Dialogue Project* featured at the Chicago Cultural Center in the spring of 2009.

High Notes is the basis of a jazz opera written by poet Lois Roma-Deeley and composer Christopher Scinto.

Thanks to the Ragdale Foundation for a residency fellowship. A special *grazie* to Martha Collins.

And Christopher Scinto, *ti ringrazio moltissimo,* for first bringing the idea for the jazz opera to me.

My deepest gratitude to Liz Abrams-Morley, Le Roy Chappell, Lesly Chappell, Leroy Hunter, Sydney James and Marianne Roccaforte.

About the Author

LOIS ROMA-DEELEY is the author of three collections of poetry, including *northSight* and *Rules of Hunger.* She has won numerous awards and honors for her poetry and has published in seven national anthologies. Roma-Deeley has taught creative writing at the graduate and undergraduate levels. She is Poet-in-Residence at Paradise Valley Community College in Phoenix, Arizona.

About Benu Press

Benu Press is a small, independent press committed to publishing poetry, fiction, and creative non-fiction. We believe in the transformative power of literature. To that end, we seek to publish inspiring and thought-provoking books about the practical dimensions of social justice and equity.

The Benu Press Social Justice and Equity Award in Creative Non-Fiction recognizes contemporary authors for writing excellence on thought-provoking themes of social equity.

The Samuel T. Coleridge Prize honors an outstanding work of literature, written by a contemporary author, that fulfills Coleridge's vision of the artist as a reconciling architect of the imagination. Such a work invites us to examine our understanding of the world, establishing new meaning in a just future transformed by possibility.

Also published by Benu Press:
Two Hundred Nights and One Day, Margaret Rozga
All Screwed Up, Steve Fellner

For more information about Benu Press:
http://www.benupress.com